C000161194

Hope
can always
be found

Becky Bishop

Hope can always be found

Poems from a pandemic year

Hope can always be found

Other books by Becky Bishop

Poetry
Seasons of Change

From the Heart

Sequins and Sparkles (Strictly Come
Dancing 2019 series)

Glitz and Glamour (Strictly Come dancing
2020 series)

War Poetry
At The Going Down of the Sun

Lest We Forget

WW2
With all my love, Melvin.

Short Stories
The Adventures of Bluebell Bunny

Facebook: Becky's Poems and Books
Twitter: Beckypoemsbooks
www.beckyspoemsandbooks.wordpress.com

Dedication

To the NHS and all keyworkers for all their dedication and hard work during the Covid pandemic.

To all the families affected by Covid

To Barrie, Carole, Rob and all at Everton Stores in Hampshire for their outstanding hard work, effort and contribution to Everton village particularly during the pandemic.

Hope can always be found

In loving memory of

All those who have lost their lives due to
Covid

Caroline Flack 1979 – 2020

Dame Vera Lynn 1917 – 2020

Dame Barbara Windsor 1937 - 2020

Captain Sir Tom Moore 1920 – 2021

Eddie Rothe 1954 - 2021

HRH Prince Philip, Duke of Edinburgh 1921-
2021

Hope can always be found

Introduction

2020 was a year like no other when the nation was hit by the Coronavirus pandemic causing the world to literally come to a standstill and hundreds of thousands of people to die. Countries were put under lockdowns, people had to work from home, children had to take lessons online, businesses had to close and social distancing, mask wearing and zoom meetings became the norm. The pandemic had a particular impact on families who were forced apart and who have been kept apart for over a year.

Throughout the pandemic the NHS and keyworkers along with health organisations around the world have played a vital role and continue to do so and their efforts should be applauded. Scientists have also worked hard behind the scenes to create vaccines which has been a major breakthrough and turning point in the fight against Covid.

For everyone it has been a time of great uncertainty, anxiety, despair and anguish although the past year has brought the country and communities closer together, whether it was through volunteering to help the vulnerable, supporting Captain Tom's 100 laps to raise money for the NHS and people following in his footsteps, Clapping on our doorsteps for Carers and Keyworkers, having tea parties in our front gardens for VE Day and putting pictures of rainbows up in our windows as signs of hope.

During the lockdowns, when people were only allowed out once a day for exercise, the environment played an important role. For whilst the world may have shut down, nature came alive and hopefully this has taught us to appreciate the environment more, the beauty of nature and the benefits it can have on our well-being and mental health.

With the vaccine drive in full swing, restrictions lifting and families now able to reunite, things are at last looking more positive and people can finally have hope that better times are on the way.

The past year and a half has not only seen thousands tragically die from Covid but has also seen the tragic deaths of several high profile people, such as Caroline Flack, Dame Vera Lynn, Dame Barbara Windsor, Captain Sir Tom Moore and HRH Prince Philip.

2020 and the first half of 2021 has also seen many notable events such as the Black Lives Matter protests in response to the murder of George Floyd by police in America and the vigil for Sarah Everard in the UK who went missing and was found to have been murdered by a policeman along with a Royal wedding and the births of several royal babies. There have also been many heartwarming stories of hope, such as that of Kate Garraway whose husband was in hospital for over a year with complications from Covid and who has recently been able to finally return home and reunite with his family.

Hope can always be found is a collection of poems written mainly during the last year and a half, focusing particularly on the pandemic and some of the notable events and issues that have happened over the last year and a half. It also includes poems for all occasions, poems about my local village and poems in memory of some of the well-known people who have died.

Whilst we could not have foreseen what the past year and a half would be like and although we may have missed out on many things, it has been a time that has shown us what truly matters in life. Despite the troubling times, it has shown that even when things are difficult, by coming together we are stronger and can get through anything life throws at us.

Even in the darkest times, hope can always be found.

Contents

Hope can always be found

Parents

A mother holds you close

A mother holds you close, she has you in her heart,
From before you're born, to when you are apart.

From a babe in arms, she offers tender loving care,
And as she watches you grow, her wisdom and advice she'll share.

She helps you become independent, she teaches you to be strong,
She guides you through life, showing you right from wrong.

She nurtures you with love, her love it knows no bounds,
A connection so deep, even when she's not around.

She comforts you with a hug, so you never feel alone,
She works extremely hard, to make a house a home.

We should give thanks for what she does, celebrate her in every way,
To show her that she's loved and thought of, not just today but everyday.

Mother

Mothers make a house a home and are a
constant presence in your life,

Offering love and affection, through good
times and through strife.

Teaching and guiding you, wiping away your
tears,

Helping you achieve your dreams and
conquer all your fears.

Encouraging you in all you do, words of
wisdom she shares,

Raising you to be your best, when you need
her she's always there.

Father

Fathers work hard, for their families they provide,

Achievements of their children, of whom they have such pride.

Teaching them right from wrong, instilling values too,

Helping them through life, no matter what they do.

Encouraging their dreams, as well as having fun,

Raising children, a father's job is never done.

A father is

A father is caring, a father is kind,
A father's always there, when you're in a
bind.

A father is playful, a father likes to have fun,
A father's job, is never truly done.

A father works hard, a father provides,
In his children a father, always has pride.

A father is a protector, a father is strong,
A father teaches his children, right from
wrong.

A father is a role model, a father is a guide,
A father's always there, cheering you on from
the side.

Hope can always be found

Love

Love comes in many forms

There's the love between partners or a
husband and a wife,
A love that helps them through good times as
well as through strife.

There's the love between parents, children
and siblings too,
Bonds that are unbreakable, a love that lasts
their whole life through.

There's the love between family,
acquaintances and friends,
Always there for each other, on them you can
depend.

There's the love between pets and their
owners, a love that knows no bounds,
An unconditional bond, life's better when pets
are around.

Love comes in many forms and is present
every day,
From kind gestures, to words of
encouragement and praise.

Love is about helping others and making
memories to share,
Love is about listening and encouraging and
showing that you care.

Love is not prejudiced, against race, religion
or the colour of your skin,
And when there's a choice between love or
hate, then love should always win.

Love knows no boundaries, it crosses
mountains, countries and sea,
You can't put a price on love, for it's
something that is free.

So whether it's to a stranger or loved one,
spread love in every way,
For no matter how small, an act of love can
make a person's day.

Hope can always be found

Bereavement

The Stairway to heaven

We weren't prepared for losing you, our
hearts broke in two,
Not a day goes by, when we don't think of all
you used to do.

Our lives now seem bereft, you've left an
empty space,
But you're never forgotten, in our hearts you
have a special place.

The red tail lights disappeared, as you took a
plane up to the sky,
And now you're looking down, from a place
up high.

Heaven's gained an angel, as you climbed
heaven's stairs,
A place where you're free of pain and
suffering, where you can live without a care.

There were clouds in our eyes, when we sent
you on our way,
We love and miss you and think of you each
day.

Grief is the price we pay for love

Grief is unexpected, when it comes knocking
at your door,
Engulfing you like waves, coming into shore.

Grief is the white feather, floating to the
ground,
A sign that your loved one, is telling you
they're still around.

Grief are the thoughts, running through your
mind,
Feelings of loneliness, that losing someone
leaves behind.

Grief are the memories, that make you sit and
weep,
A photograph, a card, a memento that you
keep.

Grief is like a cloud, that hangs overhead,
The dreams that invade, when you're lying in
your bed.

Grief are the tears, that run down your face,
The chair at the table, that's now an empty
space.

Grief are the scars, that only you can see,
Wounds on your soul, that won't set you free.

Grief is always present, each and every day,
But for loving someone, grief is the price we
have to pay.

Birthday

Birthday Wishes

Birthday wishes are sent your way,

In the hope, you'll have a special day.

Raising a glass, to another year,

Toasting to the future, may it be full of cheer.

Hearing from loved ones, who live across the miles,

Day full of happiness, laughter, fun and smiles.

A day spent celebrating, well wishes are sent to say,

You have a wonderful birthday, the happiest of days.

Easter

New Beginnings

Winter bades farewell, leaving its frosty
footsteps in the past,
A time of new beginnings, for Spring is here
at last.

The days get longer, the mornings and
evenings become light,
The sky once grey and dull, turns a blue so
bright.

The sun starts emerging, along with a gentle
breeze,
The trees start coming to life, slowly gaining
their leaves.

In gardens, hedgerows and fields, bulbs and
shoots emerge from the ground,
New life appears, bringing splashes of colour
all around.

Daffodils and bluebells, give off a sweet
perfume,
Crocus, primroses and snowdrops, just some
of the flowers that bloom.

Bees start buzzing, butterflies start fluttering
their wings,
Lambs frolic in the fields, the birds chirp and
sing.

The grass grows greener, nature comes alive,
All welcome signs, that Spring has arrived.

Hope can always be found

Harvest

Harvest Time

The nights start drawing in, summer sings it's
final tune,
The Autumn equinox arrives, bringing a
harvest moon.

Throughout the year the farmers have been
busy, sowing seeds and crops in the field,
Hoping for a harvest, that brings a bountiful
yield.

Apples from the orchard, pumpkins piled up
in barrows,
Rows of carrots and potatoes, cabbages and
marrows.

Fields of corn and maize, barley and of wheat,
All grown in order, to be made into things we
can eat.

Harvest is a time to be thankful, for the land
and all it provides,
We thank the farmers for their hard work, in
their produce they should have pride.

A time to be thankful for the rain and
sunshine, that have helped the crops once
they've been sown,
A time to be thankful for the rich earth, in
which the seeds have grown.

And at this time of harvest, we should think
of those starving and in need,
And pray that one day, they have food on
which to feed.

Hope can always be found

Christmas

December is here

December is here, a season of festive cheer,
When glad tidings are wished, for the coming
year.

When cards are posted and trees decorated
with baubles and lights,
When the tables are set, with a feast for our
sights.

When carols are sung and presents are
wrapped under the tree,
To find Father Christmas has been, children
react with glee.

When families and friends come together,
some who haven't seen each other for a while,
The magic of Christmas, gives people a reason
to smile.

But its also a time, for doing good deeds,
To think of other people and help those who
are in need.

Those who are starving and those without
homes,
Those without families and those who feel all
alone.

A time for sharing kindness, their burden we
share,
When we should show love, compassion and
care.

And let's not forget, the true meaning behind
the day,
The special event, that happened in a land
faraway.

An event that would bring, the world so much
joy,
In a stable in Bethlehem, there was born a
baby boy.

Who over his life, would spread love and do
many great things,
And that's why at Christmas we should give
thanks and rejoice on the birth of a king.

And so as we celebrate, on the 25th December,
We should take time to be grateful and the
true meaning behind Christmas we should
remember.

At Christmas Time

At Christmas time we pray, for a light to
guide and shine,
To help us through our darkest hours and
through difficult times.

At Christmas time we pray for a world, may
one day it be full of peace,
Where countries and people aren't in conflict
and war and fighting will cease.

At Christmas time we pray for the homeless
and those lonely or living alone,
May they find friendship and warmth and a
place to call home.

At Christmas time we pray for those suffering
poverty and hunger, may one day it all end,
A time for us to be generous, food parcels we
can send.

At Christmas time we pray for the vulnerable
and those who are struggling to cope,
May they find peace of mind and ways to
help them cope.

At Christmas time we pray for kindness,
whether it's shown through words or deeds,
A time to think of others and help those who
are in need.

At Christmas time we pray, to keep our faith
and belief strong,
A time for forgiveness, of those who've done
us wrong.

At Christmas time we pray for loved ones,
we've lost throughout the year,
A time to appreciate friends and family and
those that we hold dear.

At Christmas time we pray for love and
friendship, happiness and good health,
A time to appreciate and realise, the most
important things can't be bought with wealth.

At Christmas time we pray, that soon the
world will once again be filled with joy,
And on Christmas day let's remember, the
birth of a special baby boy.

Hope can always be found

New Job

Change of Career

It is a time of change, your old career is done,
You've got another job, a new chapter has begun.

At first it may seem daunting but over time you will excel,
You have a great personality and work ethic, so I'm sure that you'll do well.

Positive vibes, good luck and best wishes, are sent your way,
In the hope that all goes well and you have a great first day.

New Month

New Month

A new month is here, with thirty new days,
And hopefully better times, will soon be on
the way.

Stay safe and take care, when you go out,
For even though restrictions are lifting, there's
still a virus about.

Try and stay positive, even though at times
you may feel glum,
Always have hope, that things will improve in
the days to come.

Covid
Pandemic

Coronavirus

There's a pandemic across the nation,
Coronavirus is its name,
It's spreading from country to country, it's
gaining worldwide fame.

With high fever and cough as some of the
symptoms, it can be very similar to flu,
But if you take the right precautions, you will
see it through.

People are panic buying loo rolls and pasta,
though there really is no need,
They should think of those who are
vulnerable, instead of showing such greed.

For pasta and loo rolls, won't stop you from
catching the disease,
Instead use a tissue, when you need to cough
or sneeze.

Now our country is in lockdown and many
other countries are too,
And staying safe at home, is the best thing
you can do.

Lockdown

As Coronavirus spreads around the world,
new cases are reported each day,
Impacting so many countries, it's changed our
lives in every way.

On the daily bulletins and news reports, the
number of cases and deaths soar,
Instilling fear amongst the public, who only
feel safe behind their front doors.

Up and down the country, in all the cities,
villages and towns,
Restrictions are in place, everywhere is on
lockdown.

All the roads are quiet, as people are forced to
stay at home,
You're not allowed to see family and friends,
you can only contact them by video or phone.

All the shops and businesses are shut, the
streets are still and bare,
People are volunteering to help the
vulnerable, showing that they care.

Schools and colleges are shut, just full of
empty classrooms,
Instead children are being home-schooled and
doing online classes via zoom.

Having to use hand gel and getting used to
wearing a mask over your face,
Seeing all the adverts, for Hands, Face and
Space.

The restrictions in place, are becoming a new
way of life,
But taking precautions are essential, when
infections are so rife.

Clap for Carers

We stood at our front doors, we stood at our
front gates,
We came together as a nation, to spread love
instead of hate.

We clapped for the heroes, in their hands they
held our lives,
We clapped for all the keyworkers, who kept
the country alive.

We clapped for the doctors, nurses and carers,
looking after the elderly and those who were
ill,
We clapped for the packers and delivery
drivers and those working in supermarkets on
the tills.

We clapped for the postal workers and
rubbish collectors, the teachers and all those
keeping places clean,
We clapped for the emergency services and
military and the scientist developing vaccines.

No matter what your keyworker role, each
Thursday we clapped for you,
You've been the country's lifeline, helping so
many people through the jobs you do.

For ten weeks we joined as one, clapping for a
cause,
Showing our thanks to those on the frontline,
even though they didn't ask for applause.

NHS and Keyworkers

To the NHS and all keyworkers, we thank you
for all you do,
For in these times of crisis, the country
couldn't be without you it's true.

We thank you for your hard work and
dedication, to help those who are in need,
With no thought for yourself, you're doing a
good deed.

You put yourself at risk, each and every day,
Helping to change lives, you're making a
difference in every way.

Whether it's on the frontline at the hospitals
or care homes, looking after people and
keeping them alive,
To those working in local shops and
supermarkets, stocking supplies to help the
country survive.

There's those looking after children and
dustmen who collect our rubbish each week,
And those behind the scenes like scientists,
who a vaccine and cure for this virus they
seek.

There's the army and police who patrol and
the postmen and delivery drivers who deliver
straight to our doors,
There's also government officials and
hundreds of volunteers, to name just a few
important roles as there's so many more.

No matter what your role, all keyworkers play
a vital part,
And each Thursday night when the nation
claps, we have you in our hearts.

You're keeping the country going, hopefully
this crisis will be over soon,
It'll all be thanks to you, that one day our
normal lives can resume.

When nature came alive

2020 saw the entire world, come to a
standstill,
When a virus swept the nation, making
people very ill.

Whilst people had to stay at home, nature
came alive,
The environment came to life, whilst people
struggled to survive.

Bulbs and shoots emerged from the ground,
flowers and plants bloomed,
With bursts of bright colours and the scent of
sweet perfumes.

Nature became our haven, as we enjoyed
walks in open spaces,
Spending time in our gardens, they became
our sanctuary and solace.

Animals could leave their habitats, without
fear of humans and cars,
The environment became their playground, a
place they could roam far.

Whilst Covid stopped the world and brought
humans so much strife,
Nature could rejoice, as the environment came
back to life.

When will the pandemic end?

It's been a challenging time, one in which
many people have struggled to cope,
When anxiety and despair, prevailed over joy
and hope.

The news always seems depressing, full of
doom and gloom,
All people want to know, is when normal life
can resume.

Getting through each day, as best as we all
can,
The end of restrictions, the decision lies in the
hands of one man.

Despite keeping busy and learning new skills,
people are now becoming fed up and bored,
All they want to do is to live freely and be
able to go on holiday abroad.

When will restrictions be lifted? no one seems
to really know,
When will the shops reopen? when can we go
and see a show?

When can we go to festivals? at the moment
meeting in crowds is wrong,
When will the hairdressers reopen? for
everyone's hair is growing too long.

When can we drive further than the
supermarket? when can we exercise more
than once a day?
When will churches reopen? so people can go
and pray

When will the pubs and restaurants reopen?
When can we go for a meal, a glass of wine or
a beer?
When can we go and watch sports events?
And for our favourite teams be able to cheer.

When will social distancing stop? when can
we walk around mask free,
For when you're a glasses wearer, wearing a
mask makes it hard to see.

Most of all when will we be able to see loved
ones? meet up with family and friends,
When will life get back to normal? when will
this pandemic come to an end?

If only we had known

If only we had known, just how our lives
would change,
With an unexpected pandemic, 2020 would be
a year so strange.

If only we had known, how restricted our
lives would be,
Having to stay at home, our loved ones we
couldn't see.

If only we had known, that Covid would have
a cost,
So many people suffering, thousands of lives
lost.

If only we had known, that businesses would
have to close,
That we couldn't go to pubs or play sport,
visit theatres or see live shows.

If only we had known, we would have
appreciated what we had more,
Been grateful for our families, our work and
being able to get outdoors.

And so over a year on, we reflect on what
2020 has shown,
How things could have been different, if only
we had known.

Hope can always be found

When times are difficult and the world is full
of despair,
When you're feeling lonely and feel like no
one cares.

When anxieties are high and you see no end
in sight,
When the rain clouds gather and at the end of
the tunnel you can't see the light.

When you're feeling sad and feeling like
you're lost,
When all you really want is a hug, from those
you miss the most.

For in these times of hardship, when the
world is full of strife,
Hope can always be found, from the little
things in life.

From a friend or stranger, doing something
kind,
From staying positive instead of negative,
easing the worries in your mind.

From the flowers blooming and the birds
singing outside,
To achievements of your family, of whom you
have such pride.

From the sunrise and the sunset, that brighten
up your day,
To the newborn animals, that in the fields
frolic and play.

From a passage in a book, a story can be told,
To listening to music, helping to soothe the
soul.

From communities coming together, to help
those in need,
To people volunteering, doing good deeds.

No matter what it is, signs of hope can always
be found,
You just have to pause for a moment and take
a look around.

Stormy times won't last forever, better days
will come,
Stay strong, keep positive and have hope,
within the clouds look for the sun.

Hugging allowed

Even though masks are still compulsory and
social distancing still in large crowds,
For families up and down the country,
hugging is finally allowed.

A moment we've all been waiting for, for over
a year,
When families could reunite, with loved ones
they hold dear.

Grandparents reunited with their
grandchildren, some they may never have
met,
Up and down the country, it's a moment
families won't ever forget.

Parents reunited with their children, people
reunited with friends,
A sign of hope, that the pandemic is coming
to an end.

Hope can always be found

Notable Events and People

Praying for Australia
2019-2020

We're praying for Australia, a country being
ravaged by fire,
A country where the situation, is currently
extremely dire.

We're praying for a country, that's being
engulfed by flames,
A country suffering drought, for which no one
can be blamed.

We're praying for the animals who've lost
their habitats, may they find shelter, water
and food,
We're praying for the people, who've lost
their homes and livelihoods.

We're praying for the citizens and firefighters,
who are trying to control the blaze,
Trying to prevent more homes and bushland,
from being completely razed.

But most of all we pray, that rain comes soon
one day,
And helps dampen down the flames and fight
the fire away.

Murder of George Floyd 25th May 2020 and trial of Derek Chauvin

The murder of George Floyd, by a policeman
kneeling on his neck and back,
Would things have been different, if he'd been
white instead of black.

Held down for nine minutes twenty-nine
seconds, the police showed such brutality,
A day that clearly showed, that racism is still
a reality.

As he was held down, crying out that he
couldn't breathe,
It was a dark day for his family, for George
they now grieve.

His death led to protests, in support of Black
Lives,
If only they had mattered, perhaps George
would still be alive?

The trial of Derek Chauvin, proved to be a
landmark case,
Where justice prevailed, in the fight for equal
race.

Marcus Rashford

Marcus Rashford, an incredible young man,
Helping vulnerable children, in any way that
he can.

For when schools had to close, the risk
became real,
That vulnerable children, would have to go
without free school meals.

Marcus stepped up and working with the
charity Fare Share,
Helped to provide free school meals, showing
children that someone cared.

Petitioning the government, in a bid for
change,
Tirelessly working, for free school meals he
campaigned.

For all his efforts he's received many awards,
including an MBE,
A fabulous accolade to achieve, before the age
of twenty-three.

His hard work during the pandemic, inspired
the whole nation,
And he's become a hero, to the younger
generation.

New Year 2021

As we say goodbye to 2020, another year is
done,
We welcome in 2021 and hope it's a better
one.

For 2020 has been different, a strange and
difficult year,
A time when we've been apart, from loved
ones we hold dear.

It's been a time of hardship, loved ones people
have lost,
But it's been a time to reflect and appreciate
what matters most.

For material things don't matter, nor how
much you have in wealth,
What really matters are family and friends, as
well as ones good health.

May 2021 be more positive, may better times
be on the way,
Hope is on the horizon and with it comes
happier days.

May you achieve all your dreams and make
new memories throughout the year,
Wishing you a happy new year and sending
you love and cheer.

International Women's Day
8th March

Here's to all the women, showing the world
that they are strong,
Here's to all the women breaking boundaries
and proving stereotypes wrong.

Here's to all the women, fighting for a cause,
Here's to all the women working hard, often
without praise or applause.

Here's to all the women, against
discrimination they fight,
Here's to all the women, believing in fairness
and equal rights.

Here's to all the women, who face prejudice
and abuse,
Here's to all the women, who aren't afraid to
express their opinions and views.

Here's to all the women, who suffer anxiety
and low self-esteem,
Here's to all the women, trying hard to
achieve their dreams.

Here's to all the women, who are judged on
their gender, race, age and body size,
Here's to all the women, from the rich and
priviledged to those struggling to survive.

Here's to all the strong women, who we know
and meet every day,
All are role models in their own way and
should be celebrated in every way.

In memory of Sarah Everard
March 2021

I've been to see friends, now it's time for me
to go home,
It's only a short distance, it won't matter that
I'm alone.

I've walked this route many times, though
usually when it's light,
But surely I should be safe, walking the same
route at night.

I thought I saw something in the bushes, out
of the corner of my eye,
I thought I saw a shadow, of a strange guy.

I thought I heard footsteps, creeping and
lurking behind,
The darkness is making me nervous and
playing tricks on my mind.

Perhaps I should cross the road, or walk extra
fast,
Anything in the hope, that whoever's
following will walk past.

Then someone rushes up to me, I scream for
help but no one comes,
I realise in that moment, I'm all alone, the
stranger's won.

A few days later police find my body, it's still,
battered and bruised,
I've become another statistic and a story on
the news.

Never did I imagine, that night when I left my
friends,
I would become a victim, it would be the
night my life would end.

National Day of Reflection
23rd March 2021

365 days since the first lockdown, today we
reflect on the past year,
A time full of uncertainty and hardship,
sacrifice, loss and fear.

A year when so many people, were working
on the front line,
A year when communities came together and
people volunteered their time.

A year when the NHS, played a vital role,
Up and down the country, the Covid
pandemic took its toll.

Families were kept apart, people had to shield
and isolate alone,
Restrictions were in place and we all had to
stay at home.

Covid affected everyone, from people's
businesses and wealth,
To having an impact on personal lives and
people's mental health.

But the biggest cost of all, has been the loss of
lives,
As well as those suffering Covid and
struggling to survive.

We think of all the families, who during the
pandemic have been bereaved,
Their loved ones gone too soon, all they can
do is mourn and grieve.

Whilst hope is on the horizon, may we pause
and reflect today,
For all the loved ones lost, let's remember
them and pray.

World Theatre Day
27th March

It's been a difficult year for theatres. For they
had to close their doors,
And now they're counting down the days,
until they can welcome audiences once more.

So many shows have been cancelled, theatres
are now just full of empty seats,
The stages are still and silent, missing their
musical beats.

The artists miss their vocation, they miss the
joy of performing live,
Whether you're an actor, singer or dancer, it's
a place where talent really thrives.

Audiences miss the experience, of going to see
a show,
From dressing up and buying memorabilia to
being seated in different rows.

Theatres are special places, they have a
nostalgic charm,
And one day soon they'll reopen and we'll be
welcomed back with open arms.

Kate Garraway

It's been a difficult time for Kate and her
children, like so many families Covid has
impacted on their lives,
For over a year her husband has been in
hospital, struggling to survive.

Struck down with Covid and put in a coma
and intensive care,
Relying on medical professionals, every step
of the way the doctors and nurses were there.

Dealing with his illness as well as her job and
children, often it was a struggle to cope,
But Kate never gave up on a positive
outcome, she continued to hold out hope.

It's been a time full of worry and despair,
anxiety and many tears,
Trying to remain strong, from her children
she tried to hide her fears.

Sharing their journey, Kate's been someone
we've all admired,
For never giving up, her courage, bravery and
positivity has inspired.

Over a year on, the day finally came,
Derek was brought home and the family were
reunited again.

He's battled against the odds and proved the
medics wrong,
Whilst things are far from normal, at last
Derek's back where he belongs.

Things are looking up at last, the future looks
less bleak,
We hope he continues to make good progress
and improve week by week.

William and Kate's 10 year wedding anniversary 29th April 2021

Ten years ago Catherine arrive at Westminster
Abbey, wearing a dress that wowed,
As she walked down the aisle to William and
the couple made their vows.

A love story that began at university and has
flourished and strengthened over the years,
Always supporting one another, in times of
laughter, sadness and tears.

Since then their lives have changed, they've
taken on new roles,
But throughout it all, they've remained two
down to earth souls.

Now loving parents to George and Charlotte
and little Louis too,
Family is most important to them and at the
heart of all they do.

Supporting many causes and helping charities
in any way they can,
Connecting with the public on engagements,
over the years they've won a legion of fans.

A couple to be admired, they complement each other in every way,
We wish them all the best for the future and hope they have a wonderful anniversary today.

Sir David Attenborough's birthday
8th May 2021

Today Sir David Attenborough, celebrates
turning ninety-five,
A truly remarkable man, whose aim is to help
the planet survive.

Caring for wildlife and their habitats, the
future of the natural world is his cause,
Over the years he's worked tirelessly, never
looking for applause.

Finding ways to protect our oceans, our
mammals, our fish and our birds,
Educating us about the environment, we
listen to his every word.

A broadcaster and natural historian, to his
cause he shows such dedication,
And may he continue to fight for a sustainable
future, biodiversity and wildlife preservation.

Jordan Banks
11th May 2021

Jordan Banks, a nine-year-old lad,
Full of life, he was football mad.

Leaving treats for keyworkers, raising money
for a worthy cause,
Raising £2300 for mental health, deserves a
round of applause.

Playing for Clifton Rangers Bees, as their
number seven,
Now he's sadly gone, to be an angel in
heaven.

Even after his death he's still helping others,
through organ donation,
A remarkable boy, a little hero who's touched
the hearts of the nation.

Royal British Legion Centenary
15th May 2021

For the Royal British Legion, the year 2021,
Marks one hundred years, since the legion
first begun.

Set up after World War One, they had a job to
do,
To help service men and women, ex service
personnel and their families too.

Initially helping people from the armed
forces, with the after effects of World War
One,
Since then over the years, many hardships
they've helped people overcome.

Whether it's helping with rehab or health
issues, finance or finding a job or a home,
The Royal British Legion are always there,
supporting you so you're not alone.

With a poppy appeal each year, raising
money for a worthy cause,
Supporting the armed forces for 100 years,
deserves a round of applause.

Over the years they've helped so many and
long may this continue,
We wish them all the best for the future and
thank them for all they do.

Princess Beatrice baby news
19th May 2021

Beatrice and Edoardo married in Windsor, in
July 2020,
Due to Covid restrictions, it was a scaled
down ceremony.

Wearing one of her grandma's dresses and
with her grandparents there,
It was a truly precious moment, for them all to
share.

Now they've announced the news, that a baby
is on the way,
Their families are delighted, it is a happy day.

A time filled with excitement, anticipation
and joy,
As they count down the months, til they meet
their baby girl or boy.

Although it may seem a long way off, the time
will soon go,
We wish them all the best, as their family
grows.

Everton Village

Everton Village

Everton is a village in Hampshire but don't
confuse its name,
With the place in Liverpool, which is called
the same.

Close by are New Milton, Hordle and Milford
on Sea,
But Everton is the best, its residents would
agree.

It has a pub, The Crown, that's open
throughout the year,
Where you can get a good meal, or go for a
glass of wine or beer.

St Mary's church brings the community
together, in lots of different ways,
From coffee mornings and special events, or
simply just a place to go and pray.

Once a year in June, the village holds its
village show,
And if you need to post a letter or stock up,
the post office and shop are the place to go.

The pavilion holds many classes and groups,
there's something for people at different
stages,
From yoga and Zumba to dance and
petanque, there's also a youth football club for
kids of all ages.

There's the WI and community association,
who do a lot for village life,
From organising events, to dealing with
village strife.

There's a garage and a garden centre and a
social club too,
There's also a recreation ground, the village
has something for everyone it's true.

Everton Stores

In the heart of the village, there's the Post
Office and local shop,
Where if you're in need of something, then
down the road you pop.

Run by Barrie and Carole, they're a lovely
couple it's true,
Always happy to help, supported by a great
team too.

It's the place to go to send a parcel, buy
stamps or post a letter,
And the choice of what they stock, just keeps
on getting better.

From newspapers and magazines to flowers
and cards,
Fresh bread, free range eggs, cakes and
biscuits, the choice of what to buy is hard.

There's a range of local cheeses, meats and
also fish,
As well as all the ingredients, for making a
homemade dish.

There's fresh fruit and vegetables, local ice cream, fudge and so much more,
All of which can be found, at Everton Village Store.

Everton Stores thank you

Barrie, Carole and all those working at the
village shop,
You've been working hard each day, to keep
the store and village well stocked.

You provide a friendly service, greeting your
customers with a smile,
And to help them, you always go the extra
mile.

In this time of crisis, demand has been even
higher than before,
Especially for the elderly and vulnerable, who
have relied upon your store.

You've ordered extra stock and taken orders
over the phone,
You've set up a delivery service, to help those
isolating at home.

You've been there for the village, during a
time so tough,
You've gone above and beyond, a thank you
just isn't enough.

We appreciate your dedication and efforts
and thank you for all you do,
You are the heart of the community and the
village wouldn't be the same without you.

Sally leaving the shop

For many years you've served the village,
working in our local shop,
Serving behind the till, as well as sorting the
stock.

Always greeting customers, with a friendly
smile,
Always happy to help and go the extra mile.

Always happy to chat, you knew each
customer by name,
And without you in the shop, it just won't
seem the same.

For you've announced you're retiring, it's
time for you to go,
You'll be sorely missed, especially by all the
customers you know.

We hope you enjoy your retirement and get a
well earned rest,
We thank you for all you've done and for the
future we wish you the best.

St Mary's 50th Anniversary

St Mary's Church is in the heart of the
community, the place to go to worship and
pray,
Whether it's for quiet reflection, or at a service
on Sunday.

2020 is a special year for the church, the 16th
June is a day that should be celebrated,
For it marks fifty years, since the current
building was dedicated.

Over the years it's seen many changes, it's
seen people come and go,
It's a place where anyone is welcome,
hopefully the church community will
continue to grow.

So on this special day we give thanks, for all
that St Mary's has done,
And hope they will continue to thrive, in all
the years to come.

Gillian Thank You

You're a stalwart of the community, you've
served your parish for many years,
And to your congregation, you're someone
very dear.

Dealing with an interregnum and a pandemic,
events you couldn't have foreseen,
Taking on more duties, a busy time for you
it's been.

You took up the challenge, you've offered
support, advice and care,
Helping and guiding your congregation,
words of wisdom you've shared.

You've gone above and beyond, for that we
say a big thank you,
You've kept the churches going and we
appreciate all you do.

In Memoriam

Hope can always be found

Caroline Flack

A tribute to Caroline Flack

She was a well loved presenter of I'm a
Celebrity, X Factor and Love Island and
appeared on Strictly too,
News of her death today, came as a shock and
out of the blue.

A career spanning over a decade, she was a
star so bright,
A beautiful soul, the tv world has lost a
leading light.

Gone too soon, may her demons now be at
ease,
A life cut short, may she now finally rest in
peace.

No one can imagine, what was going through
her mind,
But if her death can teach us something, it's
always to be kind.

The angels called you home

Things got too much for you, the angels called
you home,
They wrapped their arms around you, so you
no longer have to feel alone.

Your struggles are now over, they're now a
thing of the past,
All can be forgotten, you can rest in peace at
last.

There's an outpouring of love for you, we
hope you're watching it from afar,
And in the nights sky, you're that one bright
shining star.

Your character and achievements won't be
forgotten, you'll be remembered for years,
But for now our hearts break for you and shed
many a tear.

For your family, friends and loved ones, they
just wish they could see you again,
But you can dance and sing with the angels
now, your spirit can be free from pain.

The Island of Love

The island of love, has calm and quiet seas,
It's where you now belong, where your spirit
can be free.

Free from all your demons, your worries and
cares are now left in the past,
It's a place where you can be carefree and
always laugh that infectious laugh.

A place where you can be back to being, your
bright and bubbly best,
A place where your mind, can finally be at
rest.

You'll be the morning sunrise and the setting
sun that glows,
And in amongst the palm trees, your spirit
will be the breeze that blows.

The island of love, is where you now belong,
Where you can dance to your hearts content
and sing to your own song.

You don't ever have to worry again, about
what people write and say,
For it's a place where you can be happy, each
and every day.

Caroline – a year on

Caroline you've been missed, throughout the
past year,
A tough time for your family and loved ones,
for you they've shed many tears.
Remembering happier times and your
infectious smile and laugh,
Our memories of you, will leave an
impression that will last.
Leaving a legacy, that people should
endeavour to be kind,
If only people had known, what was going
through your mind.
Now you rest in peace, up in heaven above,
Enveloped by the angels, we remember you
with love.

Hope can always be found

Dame Vera Lynn

A nation's sweetheart

Dame Vera Lynn was a national treasure, the
nation and forces sweetheart,
For during the war years, she played an
important part.

Singing to the troops, to lift their spirits and
help them cope,
In the difficult years of war, she was a beacon
of hope.

From We'll Meet Again and the White Cliffs
of Dover to There'll Always Be an England,
these are just a few of her iconic songs,
That kept troops entertained and kept their
spirits going strong.

She was an icon, a remarkable lady who
inspired so many,
Not just through the war years but even now
in 2020.

Although she's now passed away, her songs
and legacy will always remain,
And to those she sang to during the war, she
can now sing to once again.

Dame Barbara Windsor

A legend of the screen

Dame Barbara Windsor, a legend she has
been,
From an early age, she's been an icon of the
stage and screen.

The Carry on Films, saw her become a star,
And since then, her career has gone far.

A prominent role in Eastenders, seemed the
perfect part,
For someone coming from the East End, who
was a true cockney lass at heart.

Raising awareness of Alzheimer's from which
she suffered, she's been an inspiration to all
those she's met,
An icon, a legend, a remarkable woman
people won't forget.

Captain Sir
Tom Moore

100 laps

Captain Tom Moore, he's a veteran of the war,
And now for his country, he's doing even more.

For the NHS, he's trying to raise a few pounds,
At nearly one hundred years olds, he's walking laps of his grounds.

He's raised not just thousands but millions and the amount continues to rise each day,
It's an amazing achievement, he's a hero in every way.

So Captain Tom keep going, keep doing what you do,
We salute you and thank you, Britain needs an inspiration like you.

Captain Sir Tom

Today we heard the news, that Captain Sir
Tom has sadly passed away,
A man whose favourite mantra, was
Tomorrow Will Be a Good Day.

Little did he expect at the age of one hundred,
that he'd become an icon of the nation,
A true hero and legend, to so many he was an
inspiration.

For in these dark times, he was a beacon of
hope,
With his positivity and encouraging words, he
helped people to cope.

His legacy will live on, during the pandemic
he played his part,
He'll always be remembered and will live in
people's hearts.

He served his country in so many ways, now
he can stand at ease,
Thank you for your duty, may you now rest
in peace.

Hope can always be found

Eddie Rothe

Eddie Rothe

Jane and Ed's love story, first began many
years ago,
Before she became famous, on her cruise ship
shows.

Aged seventeen when she first met him, he
was a drummer in Liquid Gold,
After a short relationship, their love was put
on hold.

Years later they reunited and rekindled their
love once again,
A connection still so strong, just as it was
when they were young Ed and Jane.

Since then they've made many memories and
shared many happy years,
Jane's rock when she needed him, he always
supported her in her career.

Theirs is a love that's lasted, a love that's
stood the test of time,
And now for Jane he'll always be, the
brightest star that shines.

HRH Prince Philip, Duke of Edinburgh

Prince Philip's death

Prince Philip, the Duke of Edinburgh, has
now sadly passed away,
The nation mourns a man, who supported the
Queen in every way.

Aged ninety-nine, he's led a long and
interesting life,
Throughout it all he's helped the Queen,
through good times and through strife.

As a young man he served in the Navy, he's a
veteran of the war,
And upon joining the Royal Family, he served
his country even more.

In 1947, he made the Queen his wife,
And for seventy-three years, they've shared a
happy and loving life.

A love story that's spanned decades, it's stood
the test of time,
The Queen's companion and rock, he's been
there to help her shine.

A stalwart of the Royal Family, a source of
strength to the Queen during her reign,
Proud of his children and grandchildren,
without him their lives won't be the same.

A lifetime of duty and service, of which he
didn't seem to mind,
Setting up the Duke of Edinburgh award and
supporting charities, a wonderful legacy he
leaves behind.

As the world mourns a man, who was born
the Prince of Greece,
We thank him for his service and may he rest
in peace.

Prince Philip's funeral

Saturday 17th April, Windsor was bathed in
sun and blue skies,
As the Royal Family came together for Prince
Philip, to say their final goodbyes.

A military procession, a fitting tribute for a
naval and military man,
Before his coffin was placed on the Land
Rover hearse and his final journey began.

With his children and grandsons walking
behind, for this occasion they untied as one,
Before a minutes silence, signalled by the
sound of guns.

As he laid in the chapel, to a service of hymns
and prayer,
Despite the restrictions, it was a sombre yet
beautiful affair.

A service to honour his love and devotion to
his wife and his duty to his country and
Queen,
For the millions watching from home, seeing
the Queen sitting alone was a moving and
emotional scene.

The Queen mourns her beloved soulmate and husband, someone who was her strength and stay,
A man who for seventy-three years, was by her side each and every day.

Now she faces life alone, without Philip by her side,
But he'll be there as her shadow, a spirit there to guide.

Their love will still endure, for it's an everlasting love,
Now he can rest in peace and watch over the Queen from above.

Dear Reader

If you have enjoyed reading this book, then please leave a review on Amazon.

Thank you.